100 Days for the Earth

Åsmund Seip

100 Days for the

EARTH

Love Poetry Revolution

C/A

100 DAYS FOR THE EARTH

FIRST EDITION © Change Attention AS, 2014
ISBN 978-82-999166-2-2

EDITOR Daniel Molloy
COVER ART & LAYOUT Åsmund Seip
COVER PHOTO Filiz Telek - filiztelek.wordpress.com
AUTHOR PORTRAIT Camilla Jensen - camillajensen.no

PUBLISHED BY
Change Attention AS
Skatvedtveien 52
3474 Sætre, Norway

WWW.ASMUNDSEIP.COM
FB.COM/LOVEPOETRYREVOLUTION

To the longing

ACKNOWLEDGEMENTS

Thank you, Birgitta. You are here. For that, for all the beauty and for everything else, I am grateful beyond words. To the stars. I love you. Thank you, Elia and Lean, my beloved sons and teachers. This book, this opening up, is for you. May your time on Earth be the most beautiful one. Thank you, mamma and pappa. Thank you for *life*, for your endless support, for 33 years of trust.

Thank you, Daniel, my editor, my newfound brother and fellow keeper of the Fire. It's an honour to meet you again. Thank you, Filiz, my sister. Thank you for all the light. I could never have written this book without the two of you.

Thank you, Karene. You are a living blessing. I love working with you and my work would be nowwhere without you. Our work. Thank you, Jon, for staying true. For staying you. God, I love you. Thank you, Jarle, for being a teacher, a friend and an alchemical musician. Performing with you is nothing short of magic.

Thank you, Helene, you brave, soft, wild human being. Thank you for transforming movements and deep, healing breaths. Thank you, Zia, for it is a true gift to feel your amazing heart. May all the world hear its songs. Thank you, Pamela. You're the greatest gardener I've ever met. Thank you for your heartfelt support, radiant balance and real love.

Thank you, Camilla, for every way you offer beauty to this world, for your presence, for believing, for our friendship. Thank you, Seshen. I feel so touched by your shining light, your sensibility and clarity. Your way of dancing through life. Thank you, Line, for allowing nature to work through you. For opening so many important doors. We need you. Thank you, Grace, for your presence reminds me of boundless power and endless love. Thank you Christiane, for your open, loving arms and wild inclusion of every living thing. Thank you for tending the fire for all of us. Thank you, Pia. Thank you for listening; to your star, your moon, your heart.

Thank you, Warren. Thank you, Arne. Thank you, Scott. Thank you, Fabio. Thank you, Caspar. Thank you, Kai. Thank you, Eirik. Thank you, Bård. Thank you, Simon. Thank you, Lela and thank you, Arnd. Thank you, Caroline. Thank you, Therese. Thank you, Evita and thank you, Irina. Thank you, Sonja. Thank you, Kate. Thank you, Katrine.

Thank you, all the women in my life. Thank you, all the men in my life. All my lovers and teachers. Friends and guides. Thank you for everything you have been and everything you are. We belong together.

A special thank you to everyone who have supported my crowdfunding campaign. Together, we have given this book a flying start! Thank you!

And thank you, to the greatest teacher of all. The greatest friend of all. Thank you, Mother Earth. This is for you:

FOR AS LONG AS I CAN REMEMBER, I have felt a deep longing to get closer to life. Both abstract and concrete at the same time, it grew stronger and stronger with time, until this one day, day one, where I found myself asking the moon for advice.

A 100 days later, an even deeper sense of gratitude is all that really matters. Nothing has changed and yet, everything has changed.

Recently, a friend suggested we would end up in chaos if we all were to follow our deepest longing. Yes. As I'm writing this, the leaves are falling from their beautifully arranged symmetry into chaos and decay on the ground. Yes, chaos is natural. Yes, chaos can hurt. And yes, I will choose it again and again a thousand times in favour of holding on to the distance my life has taught me to accept as normal.

Because out of chaos grows new life. Because everything I really love and treasure have unfolded from a more or less chaotic state of not knowing anything at all. Because if there's one thing I have learned from my 100 days of listening to the Earth, it is this:

Everything is possible.

It is with this deep sense of gratitude, of chaos, beauty and new life, that I bow my head to you, my fellow human being. Thank you, for joining me here, around the fire. Thank you, for coming a little closer. Thank you, for being you. And thank you, for being here.

With love. For the Earth.

Åsmund Seip

I TURNED TO THE MOON one night. Told him I would listen. Told him I was ready to wait. She didn't let me. *Write to Mother Earth*, she said. *Write to Mother Earth.*

And so I open my body, my heart and my mind, as if the three were ever separate, to the sentient mother, my home, my muse. And open I must, for should I ever write like the moon asks, then the Earth must also write through me.

A nearly forgotten language, a way of listening I barely know. But like every other human being walking this earth, I, too, am a carrier. I, too, am a child of the same Mother and I, too, am equally responsible.

My longing is to come closer to home. To feel it beneath my naked feet, to tear down every fake wall I've come to build. My dream is for everyone to be home. But I will not try and convince you.

What I will do is to set out on a journey. Like with all journeys, I can not know where this one will take me. My hope, however, and what I set out to do, is to get closer to home. Closer to the Earth. Perhaps that will also bring me closer to you. And to myself. As if the three of us were ever separate.

I WANT TO WRITE ABOUT a bird, but I don't know where to begin. It's a robin. She lives right behind our house. My girlfriend talks to her every day. They're friends now, she says. I believe her. I look in my girlfriend's eyes and I believe she has a new friend. My girlfriend speaks a language of beauty. It's a language birds can understand with the most joyful ease.

I want to write about a bird, this little bird living behind our house, and her new friend, my girlfriend. I want to write how much I think it matters, this friendship. How utterly important I think it is. How much the future of our kids depends on such a friendship. Our future, the future of this blue marble we happen to live on. I want to write about the endless celebration I feel inside, the rejoicing waterfall of relief and recognition, the gratefulness. The gratefulness. A friendship between a human being and a bird.

That's what I want to write about. But I thought I didn't know how. Neither did my girlfriend. Nor the bird. And then we saw what was here all along.

I FIND MYSELF LOVING EVERYTHING. It only lasts for a moment, but a moment is long enough. Walking down a staircase, I can feel the steps beneath my feet. The rocks, the mountains. The wood, the trees. The planning, the labor, the care. The idea of a house that once grew inside a human being.

What purpose does this house serve? Does it bring people closer to each other? Closer to nature? I find myself loving everything. Every confused thought, every lost purpose. I love the house, its story, its people. I walk the stairs with the deepest respect. No space for critical questions. I could probably wish for a park, or even better, a wild forest. But for this short moment, I love this house as I love my own family.

I find myself loving everything. For one more moment, and then another, I love everything. Feeling the structure of life touching my body. Being moved, being the mover, being moved, becoming the movement. I am this house. I am the wood from which its made. I am its maker, I am the carpenter, the architect, the resident. I am the house, the space, the ground, the air around it. Moment by moment. We breathe together, the house and I. Walking away, I know again what I always knew. Everything. Everything is alive.

4

TODAY I TURN TO GRATITUDE. I thank the ground for carrying me. The soil for accepting my tears. I bow my head to everything, every seen and unseen part of life, for nothing is smaller and nothing is greater.

Today I turn to gratitude. To my sleeping kids, to the beds they're in, to the air they breathe. To every miraculous moment unfolding right now and right now, without my effort. Today, I bow my head to emptiness. I bow my humble head to the insignificance of my being, the foolishness of my ego and the stubbornness of god when she says I matter anyway.

Today I turn to gratitude. It's been another day. I bow my head to everything.

IF THERE'S A TIME FOR everything, when is the time to pray? Sometimes, especially in the moments after my boys have fallen asleep, I find myself absolutely overwhelmed by gravity. Overwhelmed by the world, by the human ability of making a mess of it all. The weight, the weight crushes me down on the floor, to a place where only the quiet breathing of a child keeps me from vanishing. How will his world look like? Will there be anything even close to what I call *world* today? I feel scared. Helpless. Blind.

Gravity, however, doesn't mind my despair. Gravity is what gravity does. And when I let her work her way through me, when the rhythm of a little boy's sleepy breath joins the humming choir of nature's will, my feet meet the ground and I remember. I remember. How it feels to be held. How it feels like to be at peace. There is no mess. Life is messy. But remember: There is no mess.

This is the time to let gravity do its sacred, beautiful work. With open eyes I see how my feet are touched by the ground. Crush me if you must. I am here to be touched.

North. East. South. West. Air. Earth. Wind. Fire.

Breathe in. Breathe out.

TODAY IS A GOOD DAY for dying. Today I embrace everything I no longer need. I smile to my past, my stories and my scars, I look at them as friends of my heart.

Today is a good day for dying. In my life, I dream of expansion and push contraction away. But wouldn't it be easier if both of them were invited to dance with my reality? They are here anyway. What is here is here, and everything is easier when danced.

Today is a good day for dying. I feel a wave of pain covering me like a bathroom floor full of cockroaches. Being human isn't always pretty. I am human. So I sit with it. Feel the wave. Allow any insect to feast on the rotten remains of my helplessness.

Today is a good day for dying. I choose to let go. Like everything, they say, I shall return to nature. I let go of what they say. I am already nature.

Today is a good day for dying.

8

FULL MOON IS APPROACHING. The wolves are coming closer. My body wakes up, wanting to break out of its modern cage, wanting to be seen and heard, wanting pulse and blood and sex and meat. I am hungry. I close my eyes and I see the storm, its naked rawness welling up from the inside. I am hungry and I always have been. This is old, I am old, I am the roots of the oak, stretched down into the wet soil, sucking up every drop of dark life. I am the wolf and I am hungry. I close my eyes and I smell her flesh, my teeth sink down into her soft thigh, I drown in her juice and I eat her alive.

Alive. And old. I am old. Sent by god, I join every other godsent particle in a wild howl to the raw and unlived. *Yes*, we say, as we turn to each other. *Yes*, we scream. *Yes*.

IF YOU AND I WERE outside right now, we could take some steps in the wet grass. Small steps at first, shy steps. Then, *slowly, slowly,* by letting the rain go first, our very own movements could start to show. Only you and I would move like that on the wet grass, as if we were made for it, as if we were parts of a story already written. And so we would move and move and fall into a familiar rhythm, and the trees would hum as they formed a circle around us. Supported by all that we know from the deepest moments of our dreams, we would throw our heads back and let our hands be lifted towards the sky in pure joy and ardor. For as we moved and the movement moved us, *slowly, slowly,* we would begin to remember who we are and always were. All it takes, my exquisite friend, is some small, shy steps. If you and I were outside right now, we could take them. Then, *slowly, slowly,* by letting the rain go first, our very own movements would start to show.

FULL MOON. I NEVER THOUGHT it mattered. Being cool mattered. Being funny and ironic and hip and smart mattered. Being magnetic to all signals which could make me look good mattered. Being right in everybody's eyes but mine mattered. Being a good listener, a sensitive lover, a remarkable chef and a hard drinker mattered. A good Norwegian, a solid citizen, a promising designer, a thriving entrepreneur, a brilliant writer. Making sure nobody could misunderstand my intention. That mattered. Feeling certain my girlfriend was happy and loved and getting the best orgasms in town. Becoming the perfect dad. Saying YES. Winning the argument. Being adored. Being enlightened. Being destined for something great. Being someone else.

Full moon. I matter.

THERE'S SOMETHING ABOUT THOUGHTS. I write for the Earth. To the Earth. I try to listen, to tune in. It's a physical thing. An emotional thing. A spiritual thing.

A horse can be explained in so many ways. There are atoms and molecules. Carbon and stuff. A horse has hair, longer on some places of its body, while shorter on others. It has different organs, like lungs and a beating heart. A horse has a whole range of purposes when looked at with the human eye, it can carry out many a useful task and be a great companion for cowboys and indians alike, although I like to think that being a horse is purpose enough. I'm quite sure the horse would agree.

Now, the thing is, as far as I know, a human being can never actually be a horse. What we can do, however, is ride one. We can get up on a horse and we can ride on it. Surely, there are many books discussing how to best ride a horse. Many people, absurdly enough, even make their living out of the theoretical comparison and analysis of the best possible horse riding practices.

The question is: Have you ever taken a ride on a horseback? Have you ever leaned into the experience, have you ever had the feeling that the horse and you became one single movement? That both of you depended on the other for the moment to be complete, that the idea you once had of riding doesn't reach the feeling inside of you when you ride.

Like with everything, riding a horse can be a technical, theoretical and mechanical procedure, a dry, static description of life. Or, like with everything, it can really be a ride.

When I give room and attention to my thoughts, I think of the steep cliff we humans are approaching with an increasingly high speed. I think of the despair of the many, while the few seem so attached to their substitutes for love and equally blind to the consequences. I think of global warming and political egos, of warmongering and terror. I think of how strikingly different life on this planet may be, even in my lifetime, if not to say my children's.

I think and I think and I think, and I start to feel desperate. Afraid. Sad. I feel grief and sorrow. And I believe those feelings have their place, in life and in this time. They're highly needed and I'm not saying that they are wrong.

What I am saying is that they arise from my thoughts, and if I'm not aware, I take them for granted as the truth.

Then I take my shoes off. My socks, too. I open the door and I walk outside. The grass is wet and cold, the dandelions have closed up for the evening. Quietly, I start to listen. I allow the monotone whisper from the city to be as it is while I turn to nature. I thank the apple tree for its beautiful flowers. The blackbird for its beautiful song. I thank the ground for holding me and the air for its supporting presence. I immediately feel how loved I am. How much a part of nature I am. How much I am needed, here, for the moment to be complete. I do not open up, I am opened.

It does seem like we're in quite some trouble, we humans. We're in the middle of a war, pretty much. And I dare to say that most of the war is taking place inside of our own heads. It's a war of thoughts, it's quite brutal and what we think we need to come up with is better solutions. But there is no solution. How do you solve a horse? There is no solution.

What is here is what always has been here. It is not outside of us, it cannot be attained nor acquired. It is a part of us and we're a part of it. And it can be listened to. Tuned in to. It's a physical thing. An emotional thing. A spiritual thing. Its wisdom is endless, its essence timeless and its beauty boundless. And it is always here for you. All it needs is simply for you to take your shoes off. Your socks, too. Then you open your door and let your feet guide you out, out to the wet, cold grass.

even the birds get it
silence is everywhere
without the quiet sea
there would be no waves
no storm and no fish
how beautiful dependency can be
and we all grow out of silence
silent rivers silent trees
silent movement silent
being
between and beyond
for every moment i am born again
silently agreeing
silently growing
silently
knowing
everything
and everywhere
is silence

13

THIS DAY. IT LEAVES ME ripped open. I smile and I laugh and I enjoy the easy life with friends and family. My kids are happy. The sun is shining. We're celebrating the country we live in, my home, my roots. And I feel like a prostitute. I feel torn and used and delusional, I feel disgusted and angry and really, really sad.

It's a confusing day. So many traditions, so many expectations, so much fun! It seems like everybody loves it but me. My body doesn't know where to put itself. Surrounded by festivities, and an inside flooded by darkness.

In a way, I'm just a child. If you're going this way, I'm going that way. Stubborn and unruly. I get so nauseous when the masses agree. What do we agree upon? What are we celebrating? Freedom?

This is where I start crying. I cry for my suffering friends. The mountain tops, the wolves, the bluefin tuna. I cry for toxic rivers and depleted soil. For every drop of pesticide reaching the ground. I cry for my brothers and sisters all around this beautiful planet, dear members of my beloved family, who must face endless amounts of unnecessary suffering.

And I cry for freedom. Grateful for the freedom we have, I cry out for more. It's like we talk about freedom without never having really tasted it. An ever increasing part of me feels the absence of freedom until freedom is everywhere to be found. Until every living entity on this planet, every ecosystem and every emotion, every child and every cloud, when it reaches the end of its cycle, says, *Yes, I have lived. I have blossomed. I have thrived. I have loved.*

Freedom, my soul cries out, is not the absence of war. To really be free is when every fibre of reality can experience the total freedom of being what it is. So simple. So difficult. No compromise. I am what I am. You are what you are.

This day. I smile and I laugh, but I feel like crying. I cry. Still, in some bizarre way, I do love this piece of land that we call our country. I love the naive persistence of spring, the soothing summer, the explosive fall. In brief moments of bewilderment I even love the winter. I turn to the land, I talk with it and I learn from it. My children are born here. I am born here. All of my family has lived here for generations and generations.

In the end, what is left? What do I do? I don't know. So I turn to the one who does. In my garden, some bright green shoots of lovage are waiting for my hands to guide them down in the ground. The word lovage comes from *love-ache*. My parents gave it to me. The birds are singing. The soil is dark and damp. What more is there to say.

IT IS IMPOSSIBLE TO MOVE closer without getting touched. What is a touch? The smell of burnt meat. The hair on my hand melting and curling up.

I won't get through this unmarked. Simply sitting in the grass, observing hundreds of dandelions on my lawn and the few, blessed bees drinking from between their legs, I am brought to tears from their sheer presence. How can I possibly go through with this? How can I survive this openness into abysmal separation? It feels like it's on my shoulders, that my fellow mankind's fatal misunderstandings are moving through my body for me to carry it, carry it, no wait, to sense it.

To sense it. To feel it. Embody it. To sit with it. I am here to sit with it. My whole life, for this one moment with the bees.

This is what the moon told me, when we first got together: *I'll help you,* he said. *I'm here for you,* she said. *I love you, it said.*

So I'll stay. Sit. Breathe. Trust my body, my larger body. The communion between us. Nature's ways of filling up and letting go. Breathe. Breathe. Breathe.

I JUST WANT TO BE NORMAL. A young man in his best years, climbing up
ladders and receiving paychecks. Looking at his bank account with ease,
with full confidence in his savings and his pension fund and his invest-
ments, knowing how much the value of his apartment has increased
since the last renovation. I just want to be normal. Go to work, do my
thing, be sent to a 2-day seminar on more efficient methods, talk about
the latest shows on TV in the lunch break. Not worry about industrial
food and pesticides and sugar intake. Worry about my girlfriend's eager-
ness to have me express my emotions. Worry about how I can make her
tolerate yet another long weekend to Barcelona with my mates. I just
want to be normal. Be a responsible citizen. Vote. Discuss politics. Pay my
taxes. Send some money every time there's an earthquake or a tsunami
somewhere else. Shake my head a lot. I just want to be normal. A normal,
young man. A normal human being.

And then there is this screaming, ravaging madness inside of me, this
shattering insanity, this wild, raw cry from the deepest and darkest
hollows of my trembling body. It is as clear a NO as a NO can be,
it is a pubertal, revolutionary sound, a refusal, a rejection, a defiance
of every artificial restrictive normality ever thought of in the history
of mankind.

But it is also a YES.
A beautiful, expanding YES.
An inclusive, patient, loving YES.
A YES from my heart. From the heart of the Earth.

And the music when the two slowly fall into the same, divine rhythm.

SILENT, SILENT, YOU CAN HEAR the rhythm. A distant call at first, reaching out through millions of roots, as if they were veins, your veins, parts of your boundless self. Silent, silent, a circle seeks to you. Wanting to be drawn by your hips and felt by the air around you. Slowly, you slip into an awaiting dance, waiting no more because you trust, you trust the movement that you always carried, you trust that you don't know and you know that it knows, you know it will guide you, you know it will hold you and move you and you know it was always there, for it was you and you were it and now you're here.

Closer, closer, you think, before the movement comes rising through your feet from below, and everything you are below meets above and soft meets hard and everything you once knew is a flooded harbor while you, you are out in the storm. The wild waves and the wind, the whipping drops of rain and the crusty salt. You are the eye of the hurricane and the great, great sky. You are the world moving through your knowing body, you are the rhythm. The rhythm, the rhythm, the rhythm.

Closer and closer. You open your eyes and you trust and you draw, you slip and you smile and you dance and you cry. The rhythm, the rhythm. Wanting to be drawn, wanting you to slip. And you open your eyes and you trust and you move. The rhythm, the rhythm.

THIS IS A QUIET BLESSING. A whispering good night, a neverending hug. Come closer, my friend, your body fits so well here next to mine. Feel with me how the ground receives us, sink a little deeper now, let us be all the trust that we need. Here we are, resting and breathing, and as we rest and trust and breathe and rest, our hearts open up to the beat of the earth. Hold my hand, will you? We have been apart for so long, for so, so long, but I can feel your warmth. You are warm. Now, a strain of your long hair on my cheek. A familiar smile with my eyes closed. Good night, my friend, my quiet blessing. Good night.

I GAVE MY MIND SO many exciting things to play with today, but now it's really getting annoying. My mind is like a dog. Tirelessly begging for me to throw the bone again. And again. Slimy spit everywhere and the persistent smell of wet fur. I wonder what's natural about my mind. How does a natural mind look like? Are we anomalies on earth's rugged face, or have we just left our dogs unwatched for too long?

The human condition never stops puzzling me. When did it start? How did it go so wrong? Or is it actually right? I imagine myself sitting with a checklist in heaven, waiting for my turn to get born. What kind of resistance do I want to experience in this life? Pollen allergy, check. Money allergy, check. Wet-annoying-dog-mind, check.

There are moments where I don't mind my mind. Where I don't try to control it. Do you like being controlled? I certainly don't. I like lots of attention and people and movement and action. And then I like being ignored. One thing not without the other. My mind probably feels the same. Only it is so used to its junkie-life on main street. Coming of age, it was practically force-fed attention. The equivalent to crack, my mind was raised on an endless stream of half digested information mostly presented as vital to get even a small shot at a worthy life. Eat or crumble.

So here I am. Slimy, smelly, insistent and a little melodramatic. On my way to bed. My body and my soul want a little attention, too. Lay down now, dog. Sure I'll walk with you tomorrow. But, beware, there will be no bones.

I HAVE TIME. RIGHT NOW, I have time. Feeling my weight on the chair. This chair was once part of a tree. I have time to recognize the tree. The seed, the earth it grew in. What was once there before the tree. Feeling my weight on the chair. Resting with every unseen detail, every complex reason and consequence. I have time for the chair. I can rest on it. Surrender my body's tension to its smooth surface, find trust that I am held. I am safe. Right now, I am safe. And I have time. Right now, I have time.

WE GET BORN AND WE DIE. In between is all the beauty. Being raised in the belief that life is a struggle doesn't make life one. Being told that life is hard, unfair, dangerous and unjust doesn't mean it is.

I carry thousands of years of brute force in me. Generation after generation of men have helplessly given in to what they've been taught. To fight. To grow up. To be a man. To be alert, careful and strong. Many of them have felt different, some have resisted, but for most, the currents have been so strong. Too strong.

And it feels good to be forceful. At least for a while. To scream and hit and command and swear. It feels good to rule. To lead and to win. It feels good to have a position and it feels damn good to use it.

When I lose it with my kids, when my clouds get really dark and my anger takes all the space, when I hit my fist in the table or shout at them as loud as I can, when I hold them harder than I want to, and harder than they want to, when I do those things, and more, the truth is – I am helpless. My body is full of pain. A thunderstorm in my stomach, rusty nails in my heart. But I can't feel it. If I felt it, I would immediately come to a stop, sit down and cry.

It is my pain. It is the pain of my father and his father and his father, too. It is thousands of years of brute force and it is my wounds, my programming. It is what I've been taught, as much as it is what I've not been taught. It is my pain. And the only thing bringing me closer to myself and my family and life and nature and beauty is each time I'm able to stop and feel the pain. Notice it as it happens in my body. Breathe into it. Sit with it. Feel how it moves around in my torso, how it threatens to rip me apart, how it sometimes does and I cry as have I never cried before. But I do not die. I live. More and more.

We get born and we die. In between is all the beauty. And all the pain. Life, the experience of being alive, and not only a reactive piece of software. Life. Waiting patiently for us to be real men and feel it.

IT WAS RAINING TODAY, at the flea market. Lean, my youngest boy, used his money to buy popcorn, while Elia got himself a hot dog. We found a dry spot and a pallet to sit on. Snuggled up to keep warm, we sat there for maybe 20 minutes, maybe more. We didn't say much. Lean offered me some popcorn. Elia came a little bit closer. We watched people search for cutlery and tables, old people, poor people, the couple with the Jaguar, a single mother with two kids in tow. A Polish guy with his pregnant wife. Our landlady sent him to fix our bathroom once. Now he smiled at us and we smiled back. And then life went on happening, right in front of our eyes. We happened to be sitting on a pallet, under cover from the rain, eating popcorn and a hot dog. Not much else. No great epiphanies or alien space ships. No enlightenment. No explosions. But it was some of the best 20 minutes, or maybe more, I've ever had.

I WAS WATCHING MY SON today. He fell asleep just now. I was right next to him, my hand on his back, feeling the calmness of his steady breath. Right in the middle between five and six years old. He's so big. So wise. There's not a day without me learning from him. Or at least not a day without him giving me the chance.

His mother and I, we gave him life. It feels like a strange thing to say, since he's so full of his own. I knew he was coming, I mean, I knew it was him. Long before he was born, he could already tell us so much about himself, about his needs and his character. What he brought. Who he is. And yet, we gave him life. More and more, my life feels like being in service. Not only to him, but to life itself. The life we gave, the life we once were given. The life running through us, the life yearning to be lived.

My beautiful son, my teacher, my boy. May I always hear what you have to tell, and may your life be the greatest expression of who you are. We gave you life so you could live it. Your life. Our life. Life.

Good night, my sleeping friend. What a gift you are. Good night.

23

BEING CLOSE TO THE SEA is my lifeline. My mountain is curly waves and deep blue. Every time I sleep, I swim, I give my body to the ocean, surrender to its currents. Together, we float. We become one, wet movement, the sea and I, we stretch around the planet and carefully touch the ground. Together, we hold so much. Together, we bear witness to everything, for we are the clouds and the rain, we are the morning dew and the damp fog, we are the mystery wrapped around you every day. The sea. I hold my breath and keep my head under. The mystery, the sea. The lifeline.

There is no evil, she says.
A warm wind carefully moves the aspen leaves.

WE KNOW THAT TREES ARE CONNECTED, they communicate in the most intricate ways. We know how they grow, what they need, how to shape them, and we know how to take use of them in so many ways. We know the difference between trees, we know what they're called. We know so much about trees.

And then there is everything we don't know about trees. That's where each tree begins. What does an old oak sound like? Can your heart recognize one maple from another? What happens if you turn to an ash for advice?

Imagine with me everything we don't know about trees. Imagine, and let go. Now is the time to get to know trees. It is time to get familiar with our extended bodies, our friends, our family. Yes, trees are connected with each other. And at the same time, they are also connected with us. Patiently waiting, forever loving. Now is the time.

YOU ARE NATURE. You have never been anything else. Never separated from nature, never a stranger to nature. You and nature are the same. Naturally natural. Expressed in human form. As you move around, nature expresses itself through you. As you.

You can think what you want about it. You can forget it, get lost in your thoughts, mistake your understanding of reality with reality. You are still nature.

You can deny it. You can hide behind theories and constructs, you can build cities and fences, you can chop down trees and pollute the rivers, you can remove mountain tops and fill the atmosphere with poison. You are still nature.

You can believe in an external God. You can call him all sorts of things. You can claim the only way to forgiveness from being born a sinner is to follow a set of rules given to you by a man you claim is closer to heaven than you are. You can pray for love, you can hope for Nirvana, you can devote yourself to reason. You can meditate at night or whip your back in the morning. You are still nature.

You have never been separated. Not from nature, not from me. You and I are the same. Naturally natural. You are nature.

Gifts come and go,
like the tide rushing through my chest.
I breathe in and feel the sea,
I breathe out and feel you.

An emptiness patiently waiting,
for us to join and be silent.
Be us, be gifts, be bold, be here,
be held, be loved, be you, be me.

DEATH IS IMMINENT. AND BEAUTIFUL. Were you ever not embraced by autumn leaves in every color? With a final kiss, they cross the threshold. They fall and they fall, until they rest on the comforting lap of decay. It is beautiful.

I wonder what will happen to my body. I wonder what will happen to my soul. Was I ever here? Did I ever allow myself to be touched by the ground, did I ever lay my face down in the grass, was I ever absorbed by gravity?

So many of my cells are dying as we speak, making room for new cells, new life. I am practically death on two feet, as I am dying and dying. So what do I do with my life? I am a cell in a much larger body. I am a leaf and I am a tree. The universe, in me. Immanent. And beautiful.

IF MOTHER EARTH WAS A voice in your head, what would she say? If she asked you to pass it on, to express it, dance it, sing it, write it, be it, what would you do? Could you find the trust, the hushed, loving trust that you know is there? Behind what you've been told. Beyond what you believe. But at the same time so close, so intimate, that once you find it, you will know it was always there.

You are safe, she says. You can rest. *You can stop now,* she says. Take a breath. And another. You can feel your body. Feel your legs and your feet, your thighs and your hips, your back, your shoulders and your neck, your chest and your heart, your head and your face. *You can rest now*, she says. You are safe. You can feel your surroundings, the air you breathe, the soft sounds, the ground below your feet. Can you smell anything? Taste? You can rest now. Take a breath. And another. *You are safe*, she says.

You are here, she says. She trusts you, too, you know? To her, you are so close, so intimate, that once you rest, she will know you were always here. *Take a breath*, she says. And another. Feel your body. Feel where your body meets the world. You can rest now. *There you are,* she says. There you are.

TO TAKE A SMALL STEP towards you. Then another. To come close, to meet you in a warm embrace. To feel trust as a series of tiny acts, to discover trust in your breath as it slows down in a deep conversation with mine. Your hair over my closed eyes, your body resting in my arms. My body resting in yours. The only space left between us is filled with trust, more and more trust, back and forth as a pulse, as night and day and night and day, as a gentle reminder of who we were and who we are and what once we were made of. Movement, constantly in motion, we observe contraction and expansion as our earthly selves fall back into the closeness we so intimately know. Moment by moment, as my hand slides down from your shoulders into the comforting arc of your back, our mutual trust opens us up to a larger field, a hum from below, a sweet song from above. As we find ourselves carefully swaying from side to side, we trust and we trust and we trust even more the place in the middle, the everlasting second and the deep, deep relief in holding and being held. A small step. A warm embrace. A familiar feeling of trust.

I CAN'T TELL YOU HOW much I love to fly. To trip into a flow and stay there, like swimming under water, perpetually fascinated by the light and how it plays with its wet brother, the dance of the seaweed, the gracious back and forth, the predictable randomness, the feeling of being soaked into a world previously unknown, like a visitor, a tourist, like a child would wake up late at night, rub its eyes and stumble out the door, only to find itself immersed in a parallel universe, a rabbit hole of reversed rules, a paradise for the curious and so I swim and I swim and I love swimming, especially under water, as long as I can and much longer, until, regardless what the light thinks of it, I remember that I forgot how much I also need air, *yes*, I do need air and I already did quite a while ago, but the light, you know, the light is so beautiful, and I love swimming, so I swim and I swim. And then.

WHAT DOES A TREE THINK about right and wrong? A rabbit? How can lions find sleep at night? What makes a cabbage root fly feel alive? Can you describe exactly what happens inside a lamb as it gets sacrificed?

Have you ever melted into a long hug with an animal? Felt its heart beating through the smell of its fur? Experienced its personality, its borders and preferences? Its love for being cuddled a certain way? Have you ever loved an animal as were it your brother? Accompanied it through its last breaths, watched an animal die in your arms?

A cat's advice. The patience of an old oak. A horse. Enough.

HOW CAN I BE IN touch with nature without being in touch with nature? My naked feet touch the cotton of my socks, the rubber in my shoes, the paved road. My body rarely meets the light and my mind is busy with dying opinions. Oh, how I long for nature! For stretching out an open hand through the thick mangrove roots of modern society, for breaking through the layers of man's fear of the wild. My own fear of the wild. For reaching the sun and the moon and the top of my lungs, for divulging, unearthing, exposing and living.

To walk naked next to you, to drink from a cold mountain stream, to make love in the shadow of tall trees. To follow the pulse of the wind through the leaves, to meet every part of you, not only the nice, not only the soft, but also the raw storm you carry underneath your skin, to watch you let go and unleash as I do the same and we join forces in a promised dance with the yet unseen.

To make room for the way of nature through me. Oh, how I long for nature! Oh, how I long for you! And the dance and the pulse and the sun and the light. But a hand stretched out can never be stopped. A force so strong can never be blocked. So I dance. And I live. And I scream and I love. I follow the pulse, I watch you let go. I break through my fear and I return to the wild.

34

WALKING DOWN THE STREETS OF Hannover today, I couldn't help myself from loving it to pieces. My feet hurting from all the asphalt, German cars racing wherever I turned, people shopping and eating and sweating like there's no tomorrow, noise and noise and so loud noise, the beer flowing, the punks shouting, the ambulances wailing and the Japanese tourists giggling as they gather up close and wave into the recording camera of a smartphone. I walked through shopping malls and crowded streets, smiling, as I plunged into a spectacle I rarely pursue. My body yearns for a more quiet life, for more sun and sea and dirty fingers from all the soil. Hesitant at first, it gradually trusts me to provide what it needs. It's not easy to slow down, when all you've done is run. And yet, I consider my body a newfound friend. We're learning to like each other, he and I. And so, walking down the streets of Hannover today, it's hard not to love everything to pieces. Even the shopping malls and the noise and the sweaty people. They are what they are. It's fine. As I am what I am. Exactly the same and totally different. What's not to love about that?

THERE ARE SO MANY WAYS to look upon human life. We carry within us such a vast sea of possibilities, each one of us a unique expression of the universe. Infinitely large and insignificantly small, we are capable of the unlikely and the absurd, of love and compassion and symphonies of selflessness, of travelling space and holding hands with the dying. We are so much and more.

And yet, even now, when the step from knowing all this to really embodying it is so minuscule, when we are closer to living and sharing and expressing who we truly are than ever, we still choose to look at ourselves as limited beings. We talk about human capital, we look at each other the same way we look at nature, as a resource, as a form of lifeless objects floating aimlessly in space, ready to be utilized for the purpose of economic growth.

Economic growth? Have you ever looked into the eyes of a newborn child? Have you ever closed your own and felt your breath, felt your body, felt a sense of being you? Have you ever danced, ever laughed, ever climbed the crooked branches of an old tree?

There are so many ways to look upon human life. This is an invitation to look again. You carry within you such a vast sea of possibilities. You are a unique expression of the universe. Capable, compassionate, creative and graceful. And you are not alone. Together, we are everything we need. Together with the trees, together with the dying. Now look. And look again, while I do the same. And then, together, we take the step.

I am enough. I am enough. I am enough. I am enough. I am enough. I am enough. I am enough. I am enough. I am enough. I am enough. I am enough. I am enough. I am enough. I am enough. I am enough. I am enough. I am enough. I am enough. I am enough. I am enough.

I am enough. I am enough. I am enough. I am enough. I am enough. I am enough. I am enough. I am enough. I am enough. I am enough. I am enough. I am enough. I am enough. I am enough. I am enough. I am enough. I am enough. I am enough. I am enough. I am enough.

I am enough. I am enough. I am enough. I am enough. I am enough. I am enough. I am enough. I am enough. I am enough. I am enough. I am enough. I am enough. I am enough. I am enough. I am enough. I am enough. I am enough. I am enough. I am enough. I am enough.

I am enough. I am enough. I am enough. I am enough. I am enough. I am enough. I am enough. I am enough. I am enough. I am enough. I am enough. I am enough.

37

THOSE WHO ONCE FOUND THE hippies to be naive are about to choke on their sherry. They won't know what hit them, but only for a little while, only until they start recognizing how good it feels to be loved. A revolution is coming. It is near. In fact; it is already here. A quiet revolution this time, a warm one, a compassionate one, a human one. A natural revolution. Not too early and not too late.

You can't stop an idea whose time has come. This is the time for radical self-acceptance. For looking at ourselves with endlessly empathic eyes – this is the time for saying loudly and clearly that it is enough.

What is enough? The idea that we are not enough. That we are sinners and failures and fuckups and losers. That we are dirty and wrong and stupid and ugly. That something inside of us, something basic and innate, is not right. That we have left the Garden of Eden, that we have fallen grace, that we have distanced ourselves from nature and everything natural. The idea that we are not enough.

So I turn to myself and I give myself all the love that I have. I have so much! I am so much! And I love it all. Right now, right here, I love it all.

A quiet revolution this time. The time is now. Love. Love. Love.

DO WE ALL HAVE TO become treehuggers now? What kind of world would we get if everyone would just walk around loving each other? Come on, do you really believe in that stuff? Seriously, how do you expect to make a living like that? So, who do you presume is going to make the wheels go around? Is the butter going to spread itself on your toast? You know we can't feed the hungry children of the world with organic ideologies and good intentions. Don't you know? When are you going to engage with the real society, why don't you get into politics or something? And all this sticky talk about love, please. Love this and love that, how is love ever going to make our economy grow?

It's funny how words like these would find their way underneath my skin, where they would burn like acid and leave ugly marks of doubt and insecurity. Again and again, they would convince me to refuse what I felt inside as nonsense, as silly dreams and something I needed to grow up from. To get myself together.

I'm not saying I can't feel the pain. I do get insecure and filled with doubt, more often than not. I struggle daily with making ends meet, with my conscience for the impact of my choices on my family. I know this old, dualistic world of scarcity and fear is coming to an end, but here we are, confused, bewildered, disillusioned.

And yet, I don't feel like I have a choice. Feel the pain, yes. Bear witness to it. Sit. Grieve. Cry. Heal. But then, even stronger, to say *yes*. To break my ribs apart and, as gently as a shaking hand allows, to take my heart out. To go out into the world, naked and bleeding, and say, as loud as I can, that what you feel inside is right. What you feel inside is true, it was always true and it will forever be true. And, perhaps most importantly, what you feel inside is what the world needs. It needs you to find enough trust in what you know to be true to take a small step, and then another, into the unknown. There you will get to know more. Feel more. Live more. And the world will, too.

Breathing in.
Breathing out.
Enough.

40

I LEARNED SOMETHING NEW ABOUT water today. How much of the earth is covered in it and how much of our bodies are made of it. As she gently spoke about the water, she asked me to move with it, to sense the ebb and flow of our liquid bodies, rising and sinking, breathing and dripping. I closed my eyes and met with my friend, the sea. For so long have I believed I needed to seek my friend to be with him. Now I know that I always carry him with me. And that together, we are always in motion. Now I know. Now I can rest.

Depth over distance.

A rusty nail through my heart. I thought distance was something I could take to protect myself, to shelter and nurture my vulnerable parts. A necessary step back perhaps an important room for taking a deep breath and regaining my strength. That's not what distance is.

To take distance is to compensate.
To take distance is to make an excuse.
To take distance is to submit to fear.

I vow to come closer.
I vow to see what I cover up.
I vow to feel my own pain.

All I want,
when I one day cross over to the life we call death,
is to say I was here.

I was here.

I WANT TO TAKE ALL my clothes off. Have you ever spent a thought on what would happen if you stood around naked in the middle of your city? If your only action would be to appear in the world as you once came to it? How long would it take before somebody would react, and what would they do? And what would happen if you kept on refusing to get dressed?

How far do we go to avoid feeling uncomfortable?
Where could we go if we moved beyond our discomfort?

If you and I take our clothes off in front of each other. Piece by piece, slowly and deliberately. When do you start to feel something? Before you've even started? How do you spend the hours before we meet to undress? Do you think back and forth, analyzing and regretting you said *yes*?

We are naked now. Carefully, we feel a slight wind touching our bodies. We are outside, the birds around us are singing quite beautifully and the air is warm. There is nothing between us. Our eyes meet, your breath is going a little faster, mine too. I stretch out my hand towards you and you grab hold of it. This is how we stand, facing each other, naked, breathing. Hand in hand. Over time we start to relax a little more. We both see that it is indeed possible to be together like this. Nothing happens. The birds keep singing. We are two naked human beings. It feels different, yes. But it changes, too. How do you feel now, compared to when you had all your clothes on?

I am taking all my clothes off. And never before have I felt so devoted in urging you to join me. For this is truly a time for us to start seeing each other in every way we truly are.

Out of words. Sitting with it. All of it.

What is to give light must endure burning.
– Viktor Frankl

I GOT MY RUNNING SHOES on and rushed outside to make a phone call. She didn't pick up, so I turned around even before I reached past my mailbox and started rushing back in again, already busy with what I could do next, choosing from a long list of things I should have done, some things I could do and in between also some things I'd love to do. Halfway back to the house I hesitated for the smallest of seconds. A distinct sound made me stop in my tracks. Then I noticed the first bumblebee. How wonderful, I thought, as I started walking again. But I couldn't. I jumped out of my body, got a dirty shovel and hit myself hard enough in my head so that I would sit down on the grass and shut up. And that's what I did. Then I noticed the second bumblebee. And the third. How wonderful, I thought, without moving this time. The sound came back. The bumblebees. What a sound they make! Fixed on a ground covered with white clover, I realized I was completely surrounded by hordes of deliciously furry small buzzing creatures, all completely immersed in their nectar-drinking business. They were absolutely everywhere, creating this earthly choir of start and stop and chopping wood and carrying water. I felt spellbound, I started swaying, back and forth, back and forth. What a sensuous joy, what an incredible smorgasbord of stretched time. I could not get myself away from it. And then, when I thought I could, a lonely bee jumped in, right in front of me. Now, if the bumblebees are queens, this bee was Marilyn Monroe. She took her time, alright. Sitting down on each plant like a lady, going through every part of the flower, slowly and deliberately. Not only did she make sure nothing was missed, it was as if she was licking her fingers, too, enjoying every buzzing moment as if it were her last. And then, with no regrets, she was done and flew off to her next prey. And again. What a treat, what a show. What a life. Teachers everywhere. Dancers, too. Zen masters and alluring beauties alike. What a treat. What a life.

I HAVE THE CAPACITY FOR all evil. Ask me about any dark act and I could have done it. I could have killed and molested. Raped and left bleeding. I could have performed war crimes and ordered mass murders. My hands could be filled with scars from all the punches, my clothes stained in blood and dirt. I have the capacity to close down, to shut off all my emotions, to leave compassion behind and hold my breath until the job is done.

There is no root of all evil. There is no evil.

There is life. There is us. Together, we are everything. Light and dark, low and high. I am Jesus. I am Hitler. I have the capacity for every expression of human nature. Not better than you. Not worse than you. Full of shame. Full of joy. Suppressing emotions, carrying guilt, leaning into addiction. Following my dreams, loving sex, singing in the shower.

I have the capacity to open up. To move my attention. To tap into a deeper sense of being, a deeper sense of being me. I have the capacity to look beyond good and evil. To let the two rest for a while, to trust that there is more to life than the old, familiar story. It feels a lot like walking out on a field. Grass everywhere, and flowers, daisies, lavender, too. And birds, lots of birds, supporting me with their song as my feet take me closer. Summer is in the air and the trees surrounding form a natural circle as if it were made to hold the space for just this moment. And then, as I reach the center of the field, it dawns on me that I am not alone. Right here, in the middle, patiently waiting. You were there all along.

IT IS NOT ALWAYS SO complicated. The simpler it is, the closer to truth. That is what the bat tells me. She comes every night during summer, my faithful friend. Around and around she goes, right outside my bedroom window. This way for a while, then the other way, up and then down, but always in circles. She hunts for insects, but sometimes, she tells me, she flies a little faster and wilder, just for fun. Then she carries on. Around and around. A simple dance. Precisely how she likes it.

All you need is trust.

Trust is all you need.

49

THERE ARE DAYS WHERE THE great pressure builds up until it is bearable no more. Everything comes up at once and I am gasping for breath, crushed by existential loneliness. It feels like I am alone in caring. Alone in feeling eaten up from the inside by the distance our society takes from what I find natural and vital. Anything can push me over the cliff. Today it was an invoice. The seemingly never ending pressure of earning money. This loveless petty excuse for human exchange, this sad fuck of a concept we so fiercefully use to keep each other away from each other. Fuck this. Fuck money. Fuck our economic system. Fuck having to pay money for food and shelter and everything else. Fuck our sick thirst for more. Fuck growth, fuck debt and interest, fuck taxes, fuck the total commodification of human existence. Fuck money and everything that goes with it. Fuck success. Fuck wealth. Fuck greed and fear and liberals and conservatives and socialists and every other fucking thought system that has nothing to do with nature, with human nature, with our hearts and all the vast oceans of beauty and co-creative potential waiting to come alive inside of us. It is enough! It is killing me! Because my being is not limited to this lonely, gasping body. I am every child dying of hunger. I am every murdered drug dealer. I am every desperate refugee and every unemployed single mother. I am the sand filled with tar, the unwanted weed and the overfished tuna. I am you. I am completely dependent of you, as you are of me. But instead of living that dependency, and the trust that comes with it, we choose to trust money. That is, we do not trust money. So we fight for it. Fuck the fight. Fuck all this. There are days where the great pressure builds up until it is bearable no more. Please, let there be many, many days like this. Please, do not take it. Please, be my friend.

THE GROWING WISH TO SINK down through every layer. To fall naked to the ground, to meet the arc of our story with a shivering *yes*, smeared in mud and held by roots. I sing for you, a praising song to all the mothers behind you. A humble song, a song where I bow my head to everything you are. And then we dance.

Only the night can hold this sacred space for us. Our claws force their way out through the flesh of our fingers as our bodies coil their way into a rhythm only bodies know. Your skin like the dark sea, I swim on your waves and taste the salt from your blood. It is not dangerous, it is how we were born, it is nature crying out for us to return, it is a rewilding, a rapturous breath, a growl and a howl and a shattering past.

We trust, we trust, we trust. And we turn to the earth and she turns to us. It is stunning, this dance, trembling and close. We are deep inside of it and then we are out, but it never ends when it first begins. It is close. And we are open. It is a dance. And we are danced.

I am still angry
Everyone saying I can not do it
Everyone saying they can not do it
Everyone saying there is nothing to be angry about
The bread and the circus, the hipster clothes and the fancy clubs
The right opinions and the wrong opinions
The good positions and the bad positions
The red and the blue and the green and the brown
And the discussions around them
Keeping us busy and engaged in deep nothingness
While our souls wither and our hearts forget

The wisdom in a passing cloud
A child's objecting cry
The silent language of soil
And our hair, when we return to land from a swim in the sea

When coming alive is worth more than coming to a fortune
When everything is shared
When everything is shared
When everything is shared
And everyone are saying they can do it
Then can my anger find rest
And my heart can remember

Now, my friend
Now

I have sent you nothing but angels

53

IN LEARNING ABOUT BREATHING AND how I breathe, I became aware
of how I am holding in my stomach. It has probably been like that for
something between 17 and 19 years. I remember how painful it was to
spend six months in Australia, where we kept going to the beach all the
bloody time, never a break from all the eyes and all the abs. Australia
is also where I met my girlfriend. And so, for our 12 years together, she
has rarely seen my stomach as it really is. Not because of the petrifying
size of it. Not because I am fat or chubby or overweight, not because it
would change anything, anything at all, even if I was, but because I have
been completely convinced that if she would ever see my body as it is, she
would leave.

If anyone would see me as I am, they would leave. My body. My secrets,
my shameful corners and bad habits. My addictions and my ticks. My
needs. My borders. My innermost dreams.

Deep, deep down in my stomach, there are things I thought I had tucked
away for good. Moments of not fitting in, of outer fights and inner
wounds, of accepting to myself that I am not enough. A withdrawal
of sorts, a quiet resignation. Who could possibly like and love and fall
for me? The prickly, warm sensation in my skin, rising up from my feet
through my upper body and my neck, leaving my throat thick and wob-
bly on its way, melting up my sweaty face. Who am I now? How can I
adjust to be who I should? The tears pushing from behind my eyes, while
I push back. Not now, not now. Not me, not me. Anyone, just not me.

Today. Step by step by tiny step I invite what was hidden to come out in
the light. Sometimes swiftly and like a breeze, more often with miniature

movements and respectful patience. What once was had its function. Its place. Through felt and caressed pain, small shoots of gratitude for the past start growing. All part of the landscape. My landscape.

Hold on and let go. Breathe in and breathe out. Then let go a little more. Here I am. Here we are. Learning. Healing. Growing.

THE CROWS CAME BY THIS evening. The seagulls, too. Alone and together, side by side, they brought with them a ceremony of black and white above my home, reaching down to me with their song. Together and alone. I was their feet. They were my wings. And in the sacred fire that flamed up between us I witnessed my own death. With open eyes and a tired heart I walked into the flames to be transformed into ashes and dust, ashes and dust. And so I could rise up and become the sky, I could greet the wind as she made me hers, I could slowly dissolve as I watched the birth of my new self on the ground, a naked body embraced by his mother, the grass. The soil. The earth.

I bow my head to the crows and the seagulls, to their piercing hymn for the end of all things and their humble insistence on new life, new life.

Thank you East. Thank you South. Thank you West. Thank you North.

Thank you.

There is a silence inside of me.
Inside this silence is more silence.
Inside this silence is a feeling of trust.
Inside this feeling of trust is endless space.
Inside this endless space is everything that ever was,
ever is and ever will be.
Inside this everything is me.
There I am.
Safe.
Safe.
There I am.
Here I am.
Safe.

I always thought I was special
Until I realized I was normal
Quite an ordinary man
One out of billions
More like a grain of sand somewhere in the Universe
A wine cork floating on the sea
Helpless at best
Like everybody else I don't really know
What I'm doing or why or even how
I show up and some things work out
While others are failures and fuckups
In between is all the joy and all the pain
Gut wrenching despair and god given ecstasy
Things coming and going which I mostly don't understand
But sometimes I feel clear
Like a Northern summer night
Where the sun never disappears

And I realize how normal I am
And I realize how free I feel
And I realize how special I am
And I realize how free I feel

And I realize how much more I am

And I realize how free I feel

TODAY IS A DAY FOR the unstoppable. The part of you that will never give up. Patient beyond measures. So patient, it will watch you go through life after life. Birth after birth. Death after death. Gracefully waiting, it never gives up because there is nothing to give up. You can not give up yourself. You can think you can, you can even believe you can, but you can not give up yourself. The part of you that is you is waiting to come alive. It is unstoppable and it will come alive. It is simply a question of when. Without judgement. Sooner is not better than later. You will come alive. You will experience the full experience of being you. In a way, you already are. And yet, a smaller part of you holds on so hard, defending its position as your whole and only reality. It is fine. Mine does, too. It is a beautiful, loveable part of us that makes us human. Trying to under-stand it is fine. Trying to change it and mend it and break out of it is fine. Trying to find peace with it is also fine. At the same time, the unstoppable part of you that never gives up is still here. It looks at you with curious eyes, with eyes filled with the very love you have spent lifetimes chas-ing. It looks at you. At you. And in the moment you start looking back, everything changes.

MY BOY. I WONDER WHAT the world looks like when he's my age. When he's an old man. If he gets to be an old man. I choose trust over fear. Heart over mind. I trust him. His heart. His reasons for being here, for which I am on my knees, praying to be of service. I don't know. Oh, how lucky I am to not know. Oh, how lucky I am. He is here. We are here. I choose trust, and our life, our mutual movement, our timeless moment, opens up.

59

I DON'T KNOW WHAT TO write and I feel restless. I think of what I have written and what I will write and what I should write and what I could write. I think of the book this is going to be, of how good I want it to become, I think of all the people I want to touch with it, I think of how afraid I am. Not as afraid as I once was, but still afraid, at least tonight. Who am I to claim a special connection with the earth? The voices in my head are sharp, sceptical and mean. Inside my body I feel shaky and weak. Pressure in the middle of my stomach, a lump in my throat. I think and I think and I think, and it only makes me more scared. I want to solve it, figure it all out, make a rock solid plan and stick to it. Isn't that what writers do? I need to meditate. Take my socks off and go outside, sit in the grass, feel the connection with Mother Earth. I need to breathe, go for a walk, get better at this. Someone else, I need to talk with someone, someone good and wise, someone with answers. I need help. I think and I think and I need to stop thinking. I need to find my potential and use it. I need to write in a way that makes everybody think I know my way around, and then, out there, pose as if it's true. No. I need to be dissected. Taken apart. Everybody need to see what a liar I am, what a pretentious piece of nothing I really am. No. I need to learn how to be great. How to pose, write, perform, I need, yes, I need to find a teacher, I need to read books, lots of books. And therapy. More therapy. A shaman who can send me out in the desert. Take more drugs. I need to figure out which voice is the true voice, the real me. The original. The first thought. Yes. I need to find the way back to the first thought. I don't know what to write and I feel restless.

WHAT IF YOU WOKE UP one morning with a lucid, crystal clear feeling of change. Something had undeniably changed while you slept, something had moved out of its regular place and left an open space, a confused field, somewhere inside of your body, your wayfaring wave of sensations you call your self. What if you woke up one morning and you could not point out exactly what was different from the night before, but you started your day the way you did every other, you carefully prepared your coffee, you opened the curtains and stood there with your cup in front of the window to take the new day in and greet it with your deep breaths. What if you witnessed the first rays of sunlight reaching your face as the magnificence of what had changed since your last encounter with the sun struck you, as if you could suddenly see how the story would logically bring you here, to this window, this moment, this morning; as if you could surrender to the presence living in you and through you. What if you found yourself in your kitchen, your ordinary, messy kitchen, with fuzzy hair from a long night and the promising shiver of an awaiting day at your fingertips, and you were happy. Nothing more, nothing less. The war was simply over, the searching, the longing, the yearning, the craving. Everything you ever thought you needed to be happy was present as emotions in your body, waiting patiently in line to be experienced by you. What if it was all there, all the darkness along all the lightness, all the colors of all the rainbows, and you knew you could start painting any moment, and you knew you did not have to, for every moment is a good moment to savour, so you started with the one you had, the one that was there, at the window that morning, with the sun singing delicate songs and the warm, warm coffee.

TRUST IS THE MOST REVOLUTIONARY action there is.

Trust, and I mean all kinds of trust, but most of all the kind so evidently lost to us, the trust between human beings, trust, trust is a funny concept. If nature could smile like an old man would when his granddaughter stumbles around on her shaky feet for the first time, if nature could smile like that, it most likely would. A deer needs no trust, for it intrinsically knows its place as part of a larger whole. It lives out its complete dependency of the world around it, it gives and takes in one movement, a deer knows no balance because it is balance.

Trust. When I trust you. When you trust me. When we take back our birthright, our natural way of knowing our place as part of a larger whole, when we go beyond what we thought we could, beyond what we see around us and what we have been taught. When we start trusting each other. When I can look you in the eyes and tell you from my heart that I need you. That I am done protecting myself now. That it makes me feel scared and confused, but that there is no other way than trust.

When I choose to trust you. And you choose to trust me.

IT IS TIME FOR A careful whisper, a silent song meant for your ears. *Don't give up*, it says. Don't give up. The world needs to hear what your heart has to say. The trees need it. The sun needs it. I need it. We feel your pain. Believe me, we feel your pain. Everything you feel, we feel, too. You are not alone. There is so many of us now, so many friends right here, behind you, around you. We want to hold the space for you, a living circle of natural healing and pure love, but you have to let us in first. You have to take the chance, take a leap of faith and trust that we are here. We are here. We have all doubted. And we have all taken the chance anyway. We do, every day. So, my friend, don't give up. Let us meet and sing, and together we follow the melody through the darkest night. The light is here. Don't give up. Don't give up. Don't give up.

63

I DON'T KNOW WHAT I am, but my teeth are sharp and I sense you are close. Come closer, please, I'm friendly at first. Say NO and I stop, say YES and open your eyes to the dark, for there is no light where I will take you, there is no time and there sure is no way back. What you will see is sound and ravishing movement. Your sound as we start to move, a long lost pattern of chaotic beauty, of stumbling and circling, of you hauling me closer, of me pushing you away, of us switching until we melt into the same, the same centrifugal force of claws in flesh and drops of salty blood on their way down to the earth. You take a deep breath and then another. Our hearts like heavy rain on the sea, we surrender to the waves and let them take us deep down into what we once knew. What we once were. What we still are. We don't return to the wild, we call upon the wild in us, and then we wait. We say YES. And we start to move.

IT WAS A MEMORY I didn't think I had. The sweetness, the fresh mesmeric crunch. How the carrot feels like in your hand when you rub off most of the soil, without a worry for the rest, the clean and healthy dirt that seems only right between my teeth. My boys could pull them up, and with a triumphant scream they ran around the garden with handfuls of orange gold held high above their heads. It brought me back to a time when I was the one running. I never liked the work that much, or at least that's the story I've kept telling myself, but more and more I surrender to how much I love it today. It's still hard work to like the work because, you know, there's so much distance to cover. That's the price for being human these days, I guess. Being numb is comfortable and a return to nature requires a motion going through and beyond what you think you know. I don't know. I really don't know. But I trust the carrot. The laughing children. The awakened senses and the memory I once again have.

DO YOU REMEMBER? A careful hymn or a wild wind, another pulse hidden in your chest. Do you remember what it means to be human? What it means to be you?

We women, we men, we forget. A condition we mistake for truth. For so long have we forgotten so much. Yes, it hurts. Yes, it hurts. Yes, there is a unique sort of beauty to it.

There is a promise in the air. Where in your body do you feel it? Do not mistake it for hope. Even in the coldest, most freezing part of winter, we know for certain spring will come. Spring will come because it is winter. Do you remember? Do not mistake this promise for hope. Abandon all hope and go outside. The birds are awake. The world is green and bright and filled with light. I promise you, you will not be alone. Come outside, my friend. Come. Remember.

TO BE BORN AGAIN AND again. To be kissed by the moon and reminded how small I am, how large I am, how complete I am. How complete this moment is. It would be nothing without me. Nothing without you. To come into life. It is a birth, a scream, a firm voice saying

We can do this
It is who we are

THERE IS THIS ONE FOREST. I don't think we're ever alone and so I always speak to everything alive as I walk between the trees. I say my prayers, I thank them for their uplifting presence. The rocks, the moss, the crawling roots. The ants and the mice. The dragonflies. But also the ones with no names. All the beings invisible to human eyes. I've always known they are there, I practically grew up with them, and every time I connect, I change.

I was in this one forest today. Unlike in other forests, when I'm in this one they speak back to me. Perhaps I simply listen here. Their energy is different, so different I find it almost impossible to convey their message in a language I know. They are so fast and so slow at the same time. So loving and so harsh. Playful, witty and light. Wise.

This time we agreed I would write about them. Not too much, just to acknowledge their presence as teachers in my life. In the world. They are in nature and nature is everywhere. They have so much to give. We have so much to learn. All we need to do is listen.

Before I die I want to climb more trees.

ONE OF MY SONS WANTED to know what the horizon is. We were out on the sea in a small boat, with waves small enough for me to feel safe, yet big enough for him to feel really shaky. Our first cod was bleeding out in a bucket. My boy sitting closer to me than usual, while I handled the fishing rod. The horizon. I told him it's where heaven and earth meet. The earth is round and all that, sure, but most importantly, it's where heaven and earth meet. He looked at me and I looked at him and I could suddenly see the horizon in him, or him in it, as if the elements that make up my son were visible for a second, the sacred, passionate act of love that once was the seed for what I think of as him, the coming together of light and dark, of strength and vulnerability, of magic and logic. My son is my ultimate proof for heaven and earth coming together, something so ungraspably beautiful that I am lucky even to say I was there. But I was. And he was. And is. And always will be. Because the earth is round and as we move, the horizon moves with us. And within us.

Out on the sea in a small boat. We caught one more cod. Then we went home, prepared the fish, fried it with olive oil and garlic and shared a great meal right here, at the place where heaven and earth meets.

WHERE DOES LIFE START? Where does it end? I look at the sea and ask myself of my origins. Who was I before I became me? The waves are never the same and always in motion. Like heartbeats in my ever-changing body, they reach out for the shore and think they are finished, just to return to a much greater experience. How does it feel to be everything? Had I only known myself as the sea, I would constantly long for the rugged life of a wave. No matter how short or long, no matter if children are playing in me on calm summer day or the wild rain and the wind are tearing me apart in a cold November storm. Where does a wave start? Where does it end? I descend to the depths, to the dark, abysmal fields where I drink life from the source that gives it. I look at the sea. I came from the sea. I am the sea.

BECAUSE TREES HAVE BEEN AROUND for so long, they have picked up one or the other secret about us human beings. The first secret is that trees will tell you everything they know. Trees are not shy, in fact, they love to share from their abundant source of ancient knowledge. It makes them feel alive. Not so unlike us.

The second secret is about how you get the trees to share they knowledge. This one is easy. You ask them. If you do not know how to ask a tree for something, the best way is to pretend that you do. A secret in itself, this one is most often taught by cats. Cats always know what to do, simply because they know how to pretend. Anyway, approach the tree you want to talk to and do exactly what you would have done, if you had known what to do in the first place. Before you know it, you will be in your first (yeah, right) deep and profound conversation with a tree.

The third secret is about us. Normally, trees only tell you this secret when they feel you are ready. You are ready.

From the moment you were born, the world surrounding you started teaching you things about life. Everything was done with the best intentions and much of it can in different ways be true. However, you are not what you have been taught. You are not the stories of your life, the morals you have been given or the culture you have grown up in. You are not the wounds of your society, not obliged to compensate for them, you are not the person in your passport, not the number in the statistics. You are not an economic asset. Nor are you the choices you have made, the style you represent, the clothes you wear, the amounts you can take. You are not the stories of your life. These are merely teachings, things, stuff, useful in the same way a hammer can be used on a nail, while useless in the same way that a hammer can not possibly live a meaningful, thriving and social life inside the house it helped build. You are so ridiculously much more than what you have been told. Never mind why you have been told what you have been told. Who cares, when the point is that you no longer need to believe it. You are ready. You can say NO while you endlessly love what has been. And then you can turn to yourself, to the vast, zealous fields that form a path towards who you really are, and say a loud and clear and powerful and beautiful YES.

I WANTED TO WRITE ABOUT questions and answers and mankind's in-
fatuating hunger for right and wrong opinions, but I quickly discovered
how bad I feel from the ailments of just that. Opinions. I could not give a
flying fuck about your opinions. In my relatively short life, I have yet to
meet any fox, any bat or any fish that gives a rat's ass about human opin-
ion. If you stumble upon a sorry poodle who actually cares, please let me
know. What is your opinion on life? Has it served your expectations so
far? Well, opinionate this – what does life feel like? Have you ever tried to
understand your opponent, or even better, have you ever tried to engage
in a deep dialogue with your opponent, or even better, have you ever tried
to be silent together with your opponent? If you hug someone you fear,
and you stay embraced for what is only a minute yet feels like a lifetime,
if you hug someone you really do not like, someone you detest or at least
strongly disagree with, or even someone you hate, if you hug them long
enough for your body to slowly start providing you with answers, very
different answers, if you quietly and honestly give them a hug. What do
you think that would do to your opinions? Both your breaths slowing
down. The heartbeat of a fellow human echoing in your chest. Holding
and being held. Holding and being held.

THE MOMENT YOU STOP RUNNING. The moment you stop running away from your greatest gifts. The moment you stop running away from everything you always knew you had to do. The moment you stop running away from your painted pictures of pain and misery. The moment you stop running away from joy, from talent, from purpose, from beauty, from yourself. The moment you stop running.

The moment where the moment itself is so significant you can only recognize it in hindsight, where all you get is still only a glimpse. All you know is the intense awareness filling your body, like when you can't shake the most vivid dream, as if your life suddenly got a new sound, an undertone or even a keynote, all you know is that everything is different and you can not and will not go back at any price.

Because you see. You look way behind the mirror and you see meaning, you see that life has meaning. Your life. You see the parts of you holding you down, claiming your worthlessness in a bigger picture, you see the longing for love in these desperate actions and you see, yes, you see how you can provide love and let loose and open up and start giving. Because you see. You see the moment you stopped running away from your greatest gifts was also the moment you could start sharing them with life. With your family. Your friends. Your world. The moment you stop running. The moment you start sharing.

Every breath an offering.
Every act a service.
Every moment a possibility.
Every day we remember a little bit more.

And the great love turns to us.

75

THERE IS SO MUCH CONFUSION. So much fear, terror, panic. Cities are burning, planes are falling, children are dying. When I watch the news I feel so helpless, like a little boy awake at night, searching for my mother. Alone. I feel alone and lost and disconnected. And I worry. How will this go? Why are we here? Who are these people crying out for war, war and more war and why, why do they never stop?

And the river is still there. The trees leaning with their heavy branches over the water. I breathe, I reluctantly turn to my steady breath. If I give it the time and support it needs – what does my body say?

I know what I need to be peace. So I start with myself. I breathe. My bare feet find their way to the ground. Of all the reasons, I seek towards the feminine first, towards my mother, the Earth, for I know the part of me that is her will always give me the wisdom my actions so direly need. My hands touch the grass and I breathe her in. I listen. That is what I do, my first bold move. I listen.

Dear river, dear fear. Come together tonight, for I carry you both in my heart. I look at my own war and I hold my helpless self. As I breathe and breathe and show up for the life inside of me, I open my eyes and I see all my relations. My family. My home. And the river is still there.

TODAY I AM GRATEFUL FOR the sweet raspberries. I am grateful for good
sleep and the privilege of waking up safely. I bow to my whole family
with whom I share the space on this planet. Everything connected to
everything else, every intrinsic detail I depend on to take another breath.
I am grateful for my great-grandfather, the man who depressed and tired
left everything behind to lay down and die in the forest. As he was wait-
ing for life to pour out of him, he could suddenly listen. He first heard the
wind playing with the aspen leaves. Then he heard the birds. Laying on
the ground, he found himself so filled up and supported by nature around
him and inside of him that he chose life. Or life chose him.

I am grateful for every moment I can let go of what I know and be alive.
Carried. Filled. Supported. I am grateful for being here, for every breath,
every aspen leaf. For every smile. And for every sweet, red berry melting
in my mouth.

3 Angles of love

1. The two kisses I will never forget. In the moments after our two children were resting naked on your breast for the first time. Your lips against mine, salty, shivering and warm. Your lips like something to hold on to in the long, angelic minutes of complete weightlessness, a grounding, a relief, a moment painted on the wall of time as a reminder of what our bodies always knew. Our tears, our laughter, our lips.

2. You stay. You are my greatest teacher. You stay. Not because you are afraid. Not because you could not find someone else in a heartbeat, not because you are spinning in a romantic or dogmatic story of what love is or should be. I feel you stay because you truly love me. But you also stay because you are one of the fiercest, bravest human beings I know. Because staying with someone else means first and foremost staying with oneself. Because you witness the ups and the downs, the dirty fights, the bottomless, dark despair, the hurricane of life, and you stay. You say YES to the dark, as you also say YES to the light. That is love. Behind everything that comes and goes, you are. I am so grateful, so grateful to have met you there.

3. There is so much I do not know about you. I love your mystery, I love that I will never completely understand. The overwhelming feeling of recognition, of knowing you, of having travelled through many lifetimes together, our souls doing cartwheels of pure joy and celebration. Like when we dance together, you and I. Imagine, after so many lives, so much learning, so much growing, we still don't know how to dance together! I love to feel awkward, stepping on your toes. I love the space, the respect, the way our life is a dance. There is so much I do not know about you. My feminine guide, my muse. I love you.

I AM HUMAN. I STAND with my feet on the ground and I say I am not Norwegian. Not Scandinavian. Not European. I am not white. Not Christian. I am no organization or party, no ideology or direction. I am not my background, my upbringing, my parents or my education. I am not the neighbourhood I live in, nor the clothes I walk around in. I am not my choices. Not my failures. Not my successes. I am not what you think of me and I am not what I think of me. I am not these words. And I am not alone.

I am human. I am natural. I was born to my Mother, the Earth and to her I will return. I am here. Alive. And not alone.

I was born free. Freedom is the natural state of being alive and in balance. My ultimate reason for being here is to experience myself as alive and free. I stand with my feet on the ground and I say I will never give up until every aspect of me experiences itself as alive and free. Every aspect.

I am human. I am woven from the same fabric as everything else. As I breathe, so does the sky and the swallows and the worms and the apples and the wounded soldiers and the farmer's children. As you breathe, I breathe. Alive and free. Every aspect of us. Every aspect.

Freedom is the only option.

Freedom. I am.

I AM A SEEDLING. NAKED and vulnerable I stretch my body out for the first time. I carry inside of me the possibility of the greatest of forests, although right now I will break at the slightest mistrust. That is why I need you. I need you to see me for what I am. And for what I will become. To protect me and care for me, to stand your ground and hold the space for me, but most of all to show up and witness how I evolve. When the time is there, I will share with you my fruits, when the time is there we will grow together. Now is the time for patience and love. Anything else, you know, will kill me. There is no fruit, there is no tree, there is no shadow in which your body can rest in. There is only an unspoken promise, a faint whisper, noticeable only if you let the memory of your own unfolding show you the way. Patience and love. Patience and love. Can you feel the promise, can you hear the whisper? Can you trust me for one moment more?

I HOLD IN MY HANDS an ancient pain. Like a blunt knife between our ribs it is passed on to every living man, a legacy served in silence from one generation to the next. Can I break the deal I once signed? Can I admit that I am afraid?

It has been a long time since we broke the balance. Was it fear back then, too? Although there may be many things to regret, the pain does not stem from remorse as much as from the diseases caused by the imbalance itself. It hurts to be a man when being a man means compensating for fear. What were we afraid of? What are we afraid of?

When my body explodes from the inside out in furious anger battered out on my children, I am afraid. When I use the wounds from my childhood as excuses for creating enemies, I am afraid. When I turn to violence, when I turn to porn and drugs, sugar and irony, distance and hate – when I turn to all those things that I so intensely crave to fill up my dark and empty holes, I am afraid. But most of all I am afraid when I do not know what to do. When the truth is that I feel helpless.

Can I stand still and naked in front of a woman? In front of a man?

I hold in my hands an ancient pain. Stumbling, I try to find language for it, healing for it, light for it. I stumble trying to find balance. But I try. I get back up. My heart tells me long hidden secrets of what once was and what once again will be. You could say we abandoned balance, but balance never abandoned us. It was always there. And so in the moment we turn to what always was, the feminine and the masculine will join hands in a sensuous, yearning dance.

I hold in my hands the most beautiful memory. Now is the time to remember.

I fall back to the ocean
Releasing my will to the sea
To let go
To hold on
To let go
To feel my body of salt
Stories of purpose
Wet whispers
To let go
To hold on
To let go
To lay still and be moved
Remembering my home
Waves of promise
To let go
To hold on
To let go
To see the sky from below
Grateful in the middle
My hands are open
To let go
To hold on
To let go

WHAT A STRANGE THOUGHT TO believe in, this, to look at nature over there and me, myself, over here. What an intricate web of restraining ideas, a catastrophic mistake that keeps us falling, when the truth is here, the truth is we are all here. Now. What is truth, what is truth, who cares what truth is when our Mother, the Earth, is waiting for us to return to love?

What a strange world to live in. What a strange life to live. Even when the old ideas are nothing but faint memories, we human beings still hold on, knuckles white and grinding teeth. Why this blatant fear, why resist, why resist, why resist when a wave is a wave that will not break?

My Mother, My Mother, why have I forsaken You? With the bones of my chest ripped wide open, I lay down to rest at your feet. Take me, hold me, please forgive me. Take me, hold me, please forgive me.

HOW DOES IT FEEL WHEN someone really listens to you? Does it have a name, can it be located in your body? When listening is acknowledged as something valuable in itself, when listening gets its own character, its own purpose.

The sacred art of listening. I had a conversation with some cows today. The most beautiful cows, young and strong, and curious. Cows are the greatest teachers, the wisest masters. Have you ever rested your head against the side of a cow, sinking into her patient understanding? Have you ever looked deep into her eyes and heard what she had to say?

The cows I met today told me they miss us. They miss us. That was their simple message. And with that, they reached all the way into my heart, into the bittersweet memories running through my blood, into the stinging sensations of lost oneness in my flesh, while they saw me fall down on my knees. To be separated, to be hurting, alone. They miss us.

Every day has a thousand possibilities for a heart broken open.

Break, break, break. I miss you, too.

IT IS OKAY TO BE TIRED, she says. It is okay to be weary, to feel the broken skin and the aching bones, it is okay to cry. *Cry, my sister, cry, my brother,* she says, so close I can feel her breath. Cry for the dead, cry for your loss, cry for the unlived dreams and the stinging defeat at your fingertips. Cry, now, for every time you gave up, for every time the mountain grew too big and you did not have what you thought it took. Cry your silent tears for decomposing flesh and the time you lost. Cry for your pride, cry for your shame, cry for biting inadequacy and chastening unworthiness. And cry, cry for the unbearable distance to everything you hold dear. *It is okay,* she says, while she carefully takes my hand in hers. She will never let go, and yet, her hand, it is so soft, so familiar. *It is okay,* she says. It is okay.

WHEN YOU TAKE A DELICIOUS apple in your hand. You feel its weight in your palm, how its texture meets your skin and you allow your eyes to be touched by the fresh bursts of red and bright yellow. Slowly, you lead it towards your mouth, but before your teeth can sink into its crispy content, you take a deep, deep breath, noticing how teasing and surprisingly rich an ordinary apple can smell. And then, before you even can consider how nothing really is ordinary and in what only lasts for a split second, a sound breaks the silence, a crunching, quite familiar sound, yet this time it feels like the first time because you pay attention, because you and the sound and the apple transcend into something bigger than the sum of you and that is exactly when the first drops of juice hit your tongue. You taste the apple. It is the first time, it is the only time, it is a unique moment in time that you have been faithfully waiting for since the very moment you came to this Earth and you taste the apple like you have never, ever tasted an apple before. Everything, everything has led you up to this apple, this bite, this essence of life running down your neck, and as your jaws fall into their sacred, rhythmical work, you let yourself go, you set your mind free, you melt into a dewy, delicious trust in your body, with your body, for your body, for you know that your body knows all there really is to know and so, now there is peace. Peace. Apples. And your delicious, knowing body.

Today the dive underneath

The salt, the water, the dark green,
the night had already begun
leaving me alone and swimming
almost without air but with a view
of dark sky and dark sky
and dark sea and dark sea
and me
not knowing where or how
but swimming into alignment
with the great silence

Today the great silence

DYING, I HAVE BEEN DYING all day. Shedding skin, letting go, watching lightning strike down from the sky and enter my body at the top of my head, leaving all my glass walls shattered, the ornamented barricades I once built with my blood. Who knew a head could explode in so many ways?

Time for death, time for surrendering my old body to maggots and ants and the deep, silent soil. It is time to live, and so it is time to die. I embrace my old self, I hold me close and listen to my heart's song of respect and trust, before it is time, it is time, it is time. And it is easy and it is hard, but most of all it is time.

To practice, to die, to cry. To open our eyes to a new world. To give birth. To die. To be new, to be renewed. Welcome, death. Thank you, death. I choose life.

IF YOU GO INTO THE woods and you go real slow, because all things have their own pace, and this time, the forest sings a really slow song, a hymn of sorts, one you have waited to hear and so you go really, really slow.

If you go into the woods and you let your familiar ways stay behind as the trees guide you and the wind supports you, soon you will find your-self standing in front of a small pond, a seducing lily pond, surrounded by wooden arms stretching out and holding hands, and yet with enough clearing around it for the sun to fill the entire circle with its promising light.

If you go into the woods and you stand next to this pond, say, right about now, you also take the time to listen to the impulses of your body. As you and your body slowly tune in to each other and the mud and the reed and the water and the smell and the air from above and the air from below you sink down on your knees, it is as if your body is called to come closer, to seek a new closeness with a presence you did not know existed, it is as if the earth is calling for you to put your ear down on the ground so you can finally listen, listen, listen to the whispering secrets she so wholeheartedly wants to share with you. *You are...*, she says, barely noticeable at first. You try to hold your breath to hear better, but the ground, the birds, the aspen leaves show you a different way, a breath to follow, a rhythm to fall into and you fall and you breathe and you hear what she says. *You are...*, she says. *You are worthy. You are enough. You are worthy.*

If you go into the woods and you go real slow. If you listen to her song, her devotional chant, her whisper in your ear. She will be waiting.

EVERYTHING FEELS SO COMPLICATED and messy and dirty and ugly, my mind a spinning wheel of barbed wire and dust, my body a temple for rats. The world is a junkyard filling up, a horror show, a bloody bare-knuckle fight between naked, sweaty teenage boys with everything to prove, everything to loose, everything at fucking stake. It's a madhouse, it's falling apart while I'm searching my pockets for change, it's falling apart while I take out the stinking trash, it's falling apart when I'm draped around the toilet, coughing up carcass upon carcass of rotting ideologies. What a malicious work, what an outstanding achievement, this, for humanity to make such a clusterfuck out of gold, to paint ourselves into the corner of goddamn corners, to use the dirtiest needles to screamingly inject the cheapest fucking crack all the way into our bleeding fucking hearts, I mean, what the fuck. All I ever fucking wanted was to kiss you, you know. Hold your hand in mine. I just wanted to kiss you. Walk next to you on the street, share a coffee to go on a green park bench while we make up the weirdest stories about the people passing by. Hold your hand in mine. I just wanted to kiss you.

THE TANTRA OF BLUEBERRIES. The first bite, the hunger, the unstoppable lust for more. There are more, there are many, many, so many blueberries, only for you, and for a second you think that you think no more, what you once thought was you is suddenly gone, like a drop of water in the frying sun, like a drop of sweet sweat falling from your neck down into the green moss, you are nothing, you are everything as you stretch out your hand to reach some more, you wolf them down as if you have returned from 40 days in a desert, until you stop, you stop. You sense the blueberries, their willingness to give themselves to you. You stop, you breathe it in, everything, nothing, the leaves, the crawling ants, the tall trees, the colour blue. Purple. Dark, almost black, until you squeeze one between your fingers, you lick up every exploding shade of beauty, you give yourself to the juice, the slow song of nectar and roots. The blueberries, the hunger. The unstoppable lust for more.

to leave home
to venture out, to search and search and
loose everything, to witness
everything turn into nothing turn into
a love for all things
to find the greatest space
inside and growing
a readiness, a persistance
a careful insistence
to fully experience home
to leave and search and loose and then, suddenly
to stumble into an
unfolding memory of
home, you were always
home

THE SHADOWS, THE LIGHT, the moment when the moon arrives at a complete acceptance of every phase, every shade, every unfolding movement life has to offer. The breath, the beauty, the balance. Love. Alive.

LIFE IS SO FRAGILE. I look at my two little boys, how they play and grow and how easefully they sleep. Sometimes, when I am alone at home, I go into one of their rooms and my heart just breaks. I look at their beds, their stuffed animals and their toy cars, most of them without tires because they seem to disappear somehow, and my whole body just gives in, all my defences vanish into thin air and I sink down on the floor, sobbing so hard I can barely breathe. The thin veil between life and death, the complete lack of control I really have, the opportunity we humans have to be broken open. I love them so painfully, ridiculously much, I love them as I squeeze a corner of the road rug between my shaking fingers and lament my utter helplessness, I love them as if it were the only thing I know and ever knew. Life is so fragile. Eternally significant. Everlasting and unbreakable. And so, so fragile. I look at my two little boys, how they blissfully stretch their beings, every day. I can lose everything and there is nothing I can lose. This is the heaven I am in, this is what I trust. The beautiful fragility, the ever expanding hearts.

IT ALL BEGINS WITH WHERE you are. Where you are is here. There is no other place to be than right here, where you are. A seed does not spend energy on its potential of becoming a carrot. It is too busy being what it is, where it is. Here. A seed is a seed because it finds rest in a quiet trust for life, for what wants to unfold and grow through the seed's embodiment of what is right here, where it is. A seed knows that time is all it has, and so it asks itself; why waste it?

It all begins with where you are. Where you are is here. No real need to run or fight or plan or think. This is where the rainbow starts. This is where the work begins. This is life, unfolding itself in the most ecstatic way. Right here.

I HUGGED A TREE TODAY. We embraced each other, listening to each other's pulse. As I was breathing in every nuance of tree life, I suddenly became self-aware and afraid of being seen. What would they think? A grown man hugging a tree?

This morning I got up from bed, grabbed a towel and stumbled down to the sea. Without a fiber of clothing on my body I dove down into the salty waters, and for a couple of seconds I could feel the element surrounding me completely, touching every last bit of the part of me I call my body without any shyness whatsoever. Ah, the sea. Ah, my body. What a delight, what an experience! Have you ever had an orgasm? And another one? And a different one? Have you ever felt the universe fold itself out inside of your spine, leaving you weightless and shaking from laughter? I feel defenceless against waves of shame and judgement running through me, but why, why would I stop there, when life has so much more on my plate?

To swim, to dance, to fuck, to laugh. To breathe deeply into every movement, every wave, regardless of how it looks. To get enticingly intimate with everything that comes and goes, and the vast fields of gold stretching out beyond my knowing. I love, I love, I love to hug trees. I love, I love, I love my body, all bodies, our softness, our hardness, our boundless learning. Ah, the sea. Ah, my body.

THE BURNING DESIRE, THE DEEP longing, the signs and the vague dream. The restlessness, the anxiety, the running and hiding and shaking and hurting. The overwhelming feeling of being drawn towards something bigger, something powerful and beautiful, something that feels alive, so, so alive. All of them, every last one of them, are asking you to stop. Just for a second, or a minute, or a day, or a year. For the time it takes. And then to listen. Carefully, thoroughly, to listen as have you never listened before. To your body as if it were the most precious temple. To your emotions as if they were the finest songs of praise. To your soul as if it were the space in between that holds it all in its soft arms of air. And then, allow the sea to wash over you. Drink and swim and let your tears flow, and know the river for how it always finds its way. Your way. That is all. Now. Amen.

I AM THE 4-YEAR OLD GIRL. Shot in my head, I fall down in the grass, briefly sensing how soft it all feels, before the sunshine and the crawling ant on a yellow straw and the quivering feeling of fear slowly become blurry, and I take what is to become my very last breath.

I am the receiving earth. The soil stained with blood. I hold you when you stand as I hold you when you fall, I am the soft grass and the forgiving wind. I am alive. Living. Holding.

I am the young soldier. I take the shot, I watch her fall, I close my eyes, but open them as quickly. Something wants to be said, something in me wants to express itself. I do not, do not, do not want to hear it. I take a deep breath to find focus, in a short glimpse I remember my grandmother, her songs, the wrinkles on her hands, I swallow. My throat is dry.

I am the father. I am the father with no words. A dark hole in my chest, my soul blackened into the longest of nights. I told her to come, we needed water, needed to move, needed something more, something better, something else, I thought it was safe. What is safe, what am I, where is she, where is she. I am the screaming father, on my knees, out of air.

I am the river running. The blackbird, the seagull, the moth looking for light. I am the shining stars, the universe expanding, the neverending space between space between space. I am the witness, the cracks in the whole, I am love, patiently looking forward to be expressed through you. And I am grateful, so grateful, for I may be everything, but without you I am nothing. I am the river running. The little girl. The sun shining and the ant crawling.

YES, WE HAVE BEEN LAUGHED AT. Yes, we have learned to suppress. Yes, we are wounded. But I am here to tell you this: You were always right. What you felt burning inside of you, the itch, the longing, the river pushing on – it is excactly what you are here for. What you think of as your weak spot is what the world yearns to taste, it is what we need. We want you, every living part of you, we love you, we tremendously need you to show us who you are. Who you always were. Because you were always right. And you are not alone.

I often feel alone. But I am not alone. We are many, so many people who, right at this very moment, stand next to eachother in an ever-expanding circle. We have room for you. We have room for everyone who wants to step forward and take their birthright, their own place. We do not expect you to be perfect. We expect you to be you. Perfectly strange and strangely perfect, a human with a story, a life, a childhood, a series of broken dreams and bleeding knees. A human with a desire to not only live a life, but even more to be alive. Our circle holds all shame, all stumbling moments of insecurity and triggered bodies of pain, we hold you as we are all being held. We are in this circle because we choose to be fully human. Together. This is what we ask from you, too, no less and no more.

And then, together, we wait. We turn to silence, the knowing space between us. We know that we do not know and so we trust the larger body, the larger heart. And then, together, we act.

I HAVE SPENT SO MUCH of my life feeling afraid. Afraid of the dark, afraid of being teased, afraid of not being good enough. I have felt afraid of children, of grown ups, of teachers and bosses. Of girlfriends. Of heights. Of death. And of life. I used to have a long routine of things I needed to do before I could go to sleep, just to make it right and not die. Shakingly, I would lay down all covered up by my blanket, but still with a hole for fresh air since I was also afraid of being suffocated, with my head next to my pillow and resting exclusively on the right side, facing the wall. I was convinced I needed to breathe in a correct pattern, and hold my breath every time darkness passed by my bedroom door. Exhausted, and quite sweaty, I would finally fall asleep.

As a grown man I still notice my fears every day. In myself, and in my children. In the mailbox, as letters from the government. In my meetings with rules and structures, with entrenched conceptions of social order and frozen ideologies. A fear of people with authority, men especially, with strong opinions, with a potential for violence. I carry with me a deep-rooted fear of being wrong, so strong that I sometimes wonder if this is what our modern societies are constructed from. Shame and fear, shame and fear.

At the same time, I am slowly learning how to listen to a different authority. Only, this time, it is no authority, not in that way. It does not need to induce fear to achieve anything at all. It needs nothing, demands nothing, expects nothing. It is life. Flowing through me, in me, around me and everywhere I close my eyes.

Every time I feel my fears coming I try to stay with them. To follow them through my body, to give them my full attention, to love them to bits. Not to get rid of them, not to be right. To move closer in on life itself. To embrace my helplessness, my human condition, my dark spots, and to experience myself as something more. I may be afraid. It is a natural, logical reflection of where I am and where we are. But most of all where we were. Because we are moving. We are more. We are opening. Sensing life. Flowing through us, in us, around us and everywhere we close our eyes.

I have spent so much of my life feeling afraid. I am fine with that. And now, let us feel a whole lot more.

THE STRANGEST THING IS TO open a door you did not know existed, into a home you did not know you had, only to notice how everything seems to be so, so familiar. Imagine for instance you sit down next to a stranger on the bus, someone you have never seen before, and of some reason you start talking. The more you talk, the more your feeling grows of knowing this person, of having known her for a long, long time, of having an almost eerie premonition of what she is going to say next, how she will look like when she says it, how she sometimes gets insecure in the middle of a sentence and looks at you, as if she is asking if you are still there.

Of course you are. You would not miss this conversation for the world, this magnetic field of recognition you find yourself in, drawn to this woman as was it somehow planned, part of something larger, something huge enough to influence the universe and its bewildering expansion, too big to hold in two hands, but perfectly fit for four.

And so you and your body and her and her body all turn into a resounding YES, a movement forward, a leap into total weightlessness, into vast nothingness and complete fulfilment. In the glimpse of a second before you melt together, just like the brief moment of naked clarity right before you fall asleep, you see the white, yellow light shining between you, shining through you, from you, around you, and, since there is no time for questions, you simply feel the light, you simply are the light and the light is you and so is she.

Thank you